Navigate Life's Journey

Alexandra M. Burckhardt

authorHOUSE®

AuthorHouse™
1663 Liberty Drive
Bloomington, IN 47403
www.authorhouse.com
Phone: 1-800-839-8640

© 2011 Alexandra M. Burckhardt. All rights reserved.

No part of this book may be reproduced, stored in a retrieval system, or transmitted by any means without the written permission of the author.

First published by AuthorHouse 10/13/2011

ISBN: 978-1-4567-2830-4 (sc)
ISBN: 978-1-4567-3134-2 (ebk)

Library of Congress Control Number: 2011900501

Printed in the United States of America

Any people depicted in stock imagery provided by Thinkstock are models, and such images are being used for illustrative purposes only. Certain stock imagery © Thinkstock.

This book is printed on acid-free paper.

Because of the dynamic nature of the Internet, any Web addresses or links contained in this book may have changed since publication and may no longer be valid. The views expressed in this work are solely those of the author and do not necessarily reflect the views of the publisher, and the publisher hereby disclaims any responsibility for them.

All quotations are from the Bible King James Version.

Introduction

Navigating a path for success in life can be very challenging; however, with encouragement and determination, one can arrive safely on the shores of success. This book was written with the expressed purpose to encourage and inspire the readers on their life journeys. All journeys have potential roadblocks, detours, and closed lanes; however, with hope, persistence, and determination, success can be experienced at every level. The format of short essays and poems make for easy and relaxed reading. They are large messages in a simple context, with threads of humor woven in them to lift the spirit. Although some of the poetry and prose have Christian references, the messages transcend all religions. The need to embrace love for one another and to establish peace with each other is beyond any global religion. It is my hope that the goal of this book will be accomplished and that readers will truly be encouraged and inspired on every journey in life.

Acknowledgment

"Oh that men would praise the LORD for his goodness and his wonderful works to the children of men." The ultimate acknowledgment should be to the source of all of our good. Too often people exalt and glorify themselves for their achievements in life, either not knowing or not acknowledging the source of those achievements. All honor, thanks, and praise is due to the God of gods, the King of kings, and the Lord of lords. I am ever thankful for my countless blessings and the wonderful opportunity to write this book. It is truly time now to give God the glory.

—Psalms 107:8, 15, 21, 31

Contents

God Is Worthy

God is worthy of our love,
God is worthy of our trust,
God is worthy of our patience,
Let us not make a fuss,
God's love for us is the best,
Loves us more than all the rest,
Brought us through many trials and test,
Now renews with Godlike zest,
To live a fuller life in this day,
Now don't forget to pray,
Our Lord will surely show the way.

Hope

Never lose hope when all is despair,
When there are rivers of gloom everywhere,
Never lose hope in times of trials,
When the world seems in denial,
That we are here to love one another,
To lend a helping hand to our brother,
Hope can keep us lifted,
Even when everything has drifted,
So far away beyond our sight,
That we cannot see the light,
Never lose hope when clouds appear,
For your loving Lord is ever near.

Love

Love is the greatest gift of all,
Will certainly lift you when you fall,
Love can heal this land,
And help us understand,
That we were made from love,
By a loving God above,
Let's live to love,
Love to live,
Always freely give,
Our love and care,
Always, always share.

Gratitude

Be grateful for all you have,
Be thankful every day,
For you know not the hour it all will fly away,
Are you aware of your blessings?
Are you grateful for them?
Are you only aware of the dressings?
The borders and outer trim?
Live in thankfulness to God daily,
Worthy to be thanked and praised,
Let an endless song of joy and gladness
Be forever raised.

Celebration

Make every day of life a celebration,
Don't wait for calendar events of a nation,
Get up each day like a child at play,
Blow those blues bubbles far away,
Put a great smile on your face,
Let joy and laughter take sorrow's place,
Let celebration of life be part of you,
To lift you, cheer you, and make you new.

Blooming

You are blooming with your flowers,
They are everywhere,
Have no fear of April showers,
Have no concern or care,
You are blooming with your flowers,
Yes, it's time to cheer,
Time to cherish all of the hours,
Spring is drawing near,
You are blooming with your flowers,
One petal at a time,
Open up each day and greet the warm sunshine,
You are blooming with your flowers,
What beauty to behold,
How glorious and wonderful,
Priceless beyond fine gold.

Laughter

"Laughter is the music of the soul,"
An ancient Chinese proverb said,
A soul that is truly alive,
Full of spirit, full of life,
Never in a state of dread,
Let your laughter shift you up instead,
To a place where your spirit is free,
Let it shake off the sadness,
Put on the face of gladness,
Stand up straight now and be,
Laugh out loud—it's contagious,
The dead will say you are outrageous,
Don't be concerned,
They have their lessons to learn,
Let laughter bring you alive daily,
Even if it is at yourself,
Pick a praise song and sing it all day,
Now that will keep all devilments at bay,
Let your laughter be your shield,
It will insure you of a wonderful day.

The Little Child

The little child has all the gifts,
Ready to go out to play,
Does not care about the rain,
Playful, joyful, and free,
This is how we should be,
Let us find that little child,
Inside of you and me,
Let's go out to play together,
No matter what the weather,
Let's share our gifts of joy and laughter,
Then we will live happily ever after,
Seek the little child in you today,
Then go out to play, play, play.

Look In Your Own Mirror

Look in your own mirror,
Look how special you are,
Look in your own mirror,
You don't have to look far,
To see how lovely you are,
The world says look at others,
God says look under the covers,
There your eternal blessedness,
Your internal loveliness is so much more,
The outer shell is fading fast,
The clock is ticking on that door,
Your eternal internal made to last.

Royalty

Born of royal blood,
Our savior and our Lord,
Born in poverty for you and me,
Born to suffer and die for us,
So that we might be free,
True royalty is not a garment,
An outfit you put on,
It is God's royal nature within you,
Waiting to be born,
The world is lost in pomp and circumstance,
Royalty is an inside job,
Will you give our Lord a chance,
To fit you for his crown,
Then you will stand taller,
Never again will you be down.

Get Lifted By Enthusiasm

What are you enthused about today?
Or is it just another roll-the-videotape-Gerry day?
What will get your spirits soaring?
Or is your life pretty boring?
The power is in your hands
To make a grand stand
So get up and strike up the band
Blow your bugle and fife
It's another glorious day of life

You Will Rise

In the midst of the storm, you will rise,
In the blazing flame, you will rise,
In the roaring wind, you will rise,
Trouble all around, you will rise,
No friends, you rise,
Misunderstood, you will rise,
Rejected, you will rise,
In despair, you will rise,
From ashes to victory,
Soaring like an eagle high above the tree,
Farther than the eye can see,
The sad shadows of your past have moved away,
Now enjoy this sunny bright new day.

A Time For Healing

Too much suffering,
Too much pain,
Let not our tears be in vain,
A time for healing must come in the land,
A time for people to take a stand,
Stand for what is just, what is right and true,
Even if you are among the few,
You need not the crowd to deliver the message,
To bring healing to the land,
For survival of this age.

The Healing Smile

A simple smile can lift a soul and restore it to new life,
Open up and share yours daily with everyone you meet,
Smiling from a soul that has no bitterness or strife,
Have your great smile ready for everyone you greet,
The healing smile may cheer a soul that's down and in retreat,
It will resurrect their spirit and lift it from defeat,
Just share your smile and watch them come alive,
Yes, the healing smile can heal and even revive.

Know The Value Of Kindness

Know the value of kindness,
It will take you a long way,
Know the value of kindness,
It will teach you what to say,
Know the value of kindness,
You will not go astray,
Know the value of kindness,
Share it every day,
Know the value of kindness,
It is truly the way,
Know the value of kindness,
Let's start today.

Mental Navigation

Sail the high seas of your mind,
There is a memory you need to find,
The one that remembers love,
The kind that comes from above,
Steer to the east a little bit more,
You may find it near a shore,
An eternal open door,
The arms of Jesus outstretched to you,
Gently waiting to make you new.

The Best Things In Life Are Free

The best things in life are free,
God gave them to you and me,
A beautiful sunrise,
A beautiful sunset,
A blooming meadow,
So lovely to see,
The best things in life are free,
Consider the strong oak tree,
Consider the rose and the lily,
The best things in life are free,
Given by our creator to you and me.

Thanksgiving Day

Thanksgiving Day is not a meal you eat, nor is it just a delicious treat.
It is a day like any other when we should give thanks.
Thankful to God for all of our daily benefits and blessings,
Not just for the stuffing and the dressing,
Better to be full of the source of it all,
Than to be full of the sauce if it all,
The sauce will go in one end and out the other,
The source can remain with you forever,
Giving us reason to be thankful and glad,
Knowing of God's constant love, surely you can't be sad,
Share your turkey, sauce, pies, and cake,
With a needy family, what smiles you will make,
Share the laughs, share the fun,
Let Thanksgiving Day be daily for everyone.

Yes, I Can

Yes, I can love all for Jesus,
I can give them smiles they need,
Yes, I can love all for Jesus,
For he suffered and died for me,
One special day on calvary,
Yes, I can love all for Jesus,
For he has set me free.

For Such A Time As This

For such a time as this I was born,
In a world broken and torn,
Here to share the way, the life,
Here to help mend the strife,
Love is missing from the equation,
The world and the nation,
The energy of love most powerful of all,
Will surely restore us from the fall,
Let each person extend a loving hand,
To your fellow man and woman,
Open your heart a little more each day,
Watch the clouds melt away,
Oh, sweet love forever stay.

Anchor

Arrived at your destination I see,
How truly joyful you must be,
What will secure your arrival?
Will you float back out to sea?
You will now need your anchor,
Or will success just float away?
Be anchored in Christ Jesus,
Your success will forever stay,
Be anchored in the word of God,
There is now no price to pay,
Jesus paid that price on calvary,
To make you forever free,
His anchor will hold your success,
In everything you do,
You need not settle for anything less,
Than God's ultimate best for you,
Be anchored in his love,
Be anchored in his peace,
Your soul will soar like a dove,
So joyful in release,
Glowing in love from above.

Live From Love

The life lived from love is open, free, exciting, and constantly flowering. The word alone will direct your spirit to a higher place within you. The word can be employed to diminish dislike for something you don't care to do. If it is something that you would like to incorporate in your routine, just keep repeating that you love it until you really do. Repeat the word over and over in your day, an exercise that will lighten and lift your spirit. The word itself has the highest vibration in the universe, the highest energy source ever. Daily apply your love cream whether shaving or cleaning your face. As you smooth it on your skin, speak within yourself the word "love" or the saying "I love you." Unless you love who you are first, it will be difficult to love others. Embrace yourself every day. Smile into your own mirror when you don't encounter someone else smiling at you during the day. To live from love is to live from a truthful place within yourself. First, being true to yourself is vital to being true to others. Any division from within impedes the harmony love brings. Living from love can be a challenge when the mind is ruling you and not serving you. Try not to get locked into just doing. Establish your being before the mind start its programs. God's love is the greatest love of all, and embracing the ultimate gift of his son's love is heaven on earth. Jesus taught us the message of divine love, which is the highest level of love. This love carries the highest vibration, because it loves for love's sake and it does not seek love in return. May you receive the courage you need to live from love and become the love you do not see.

Jesus, The Love Sacrifice

Jesus was born into the world for one purpose alone, and that was to save mankind from the sinful nature of destruction. The second Adam, a living spirit embodied by his father and mother to save mankind, gave his life for others. The magnitude of his sacrifice is immeasurable, uncountable, and utterly beyond human understanding. God's love for his people is truly revealed through the sacrifice of his son on the cross. The ultimate love gift to the world to restore, revive, and renew all that would receive his son as their savior. Through his sacrifice, there was total reversal of the curse of the first Adam. The material world looks for perks and advantages; however, they have missed the greatest perks of all. With Jesus as their savior, let's see now there's the gift of eternal life, the gift of forgiveness for past misdeeds, the power and authority to rule here, complete health, peace, joy, wealth, all of which is connected to the source of all your needs, and last but not least, love. Wow! Now that's Christmas every day and reason to celebrate the King of kings and the Lord of lords.

The Higher Nature

The complexity of human nature does not dismiss our necessity to understand various aspects of the nature. It is really not so complex as one may think, especially when it is understood from the character content of each nature. The higher nature of our being is caring, peaceful, charitable, kind, loving, and forgiving. The lower nature, of course, is the complete opposite. Hence, there is the downward spiral of mind, body, and soul we often encounter. The higher nature harnesses the positive energy, the lower nature harnesses negative energy. It is very important that you build your higher nature with more positive actions in life in order to manifest your positive energy field. Embrace your own higher nature as much as possible, even if you are not acknowledged for it. Some will connect with your positive energy. Some won't have a clue. This should never negate the importance of establishing your higher nature for well-being. It is too powerful and important to dismiss today, especially when we see so many who are impoverished in this area. There is an inner battle that you must fight to win. On some days, you may give the person who annoys you a piece of your mind. On other days, you may be sunshine with cupcakes. The tug-of-war between one aspect of your nature and the other may seem endless; however, once you have decided for your higher nature, you will always win. It is the role of the lower nature to put up the best fight it can before you permanently shift upward. Stay encouraged during this process, and you will see victory.

Live Your Best Life Now

One would believe that their best life is lived from what they possess, their financial status, and possibly social standing. Certainly, these factors should not be excluded completely; however, they are all trees in the backyard. They are outside of you. Your best life is lived from an evolutionary process from within you, drawing you closer to a deeper wealth within yourself. The wealth of character, completeness, and contentment as well as temporal material success must be your goals. Your best life will be lived from love—love for the creator, love for others, and love for yourself. The energy of love elevates you, heals you, and restores all to harmony. Through the power of love, you begin to climb the ladder of spiritual evolution as your higher nature is awakened. Negative energies are being starved rather than fed as positive energies are now replacing them, bringing new peace and calm. Your best life will be lived from kindness and the amazing power that accompanies it. Kindness restores harmony and builds positive energy within you. You will benefit more than the person who is the recipient of your kind deeds. Your best life will be lived from laughter. It can diffuse negative people as well as atmospheres and propel your spirit to the stars. Look for something to laugh at each day. Focus your attention away from the disturbing news reports and newspapers that drain your joy and laughter. Replace these experiences with good songs for the day or good jokes that make you laugh. Your best life will be lived from peace. In the daily, active world, you are constantly bombarded with noise. It is literally everywhere you go; however, the absence of external noise is not true peace. True peace comes from within you. When you are at peace with God, oneself, and your fellow man, you will have true peace. Jesus came to restore that peace to mankind and to heal divisions and conflicts. It is now each individual's choice to embrace that peace for him or herself. Your best life will be lived from joy, a joy not dependent on outer events or circumstances, yet a perpetual inner state that is constant. This joy comes from God only, a precious gift reserved for those who are obedient to his will. Temporal treasures are temporal pleasures, and the cycle starts over and over again. You can finally get off the wheel when you can say, "I have been there and done that." Seek the eternal joy that comes from our Lord. The best life is lived from forgiveness. Forgiveness frees you from the past and clears the way for a greater future. We are not truly successful when unresolved issues of the past tower over us. Forgiveness is not an easy task. Therefore, your prayers to your Holy Spirit are imperative. Martin Luther King, Jr., stated, "Forgiveness is not just an occasional act: It is a permanent attitude." This attitude of forgiveness keeps your temple clear and clean to receive God's blessings. Forgiving forward gives you great peace, contentment, and inner strength. As the traditional version of The Lord's Prayer says, "Forgive us our trespasses as we forgive those who trespass against us." Live your best life now from the wellsprings of your glorious inner being, and yes, you may also enjoy whatever your favorites are and live life to its fullest.

Priceless Hope

The value of hope is priceless, far beyond what is hoped for. Without hope, we merely exist from day to day, aimlessly going through the motions. Faith and hope give you expectancy for what it is you hope for. Being hopeful for the good in your life keeps you alive inside, even in the face of hopelessness. Don't let fear rob you of your hopes and dreams and make a casualty of your spirit when you are buried. Bring them alive now. Go for your dreams with every breath you have in your being. As soon as you get your head and your heart lined up, you will be on your way. First your mind decides what it is you hope for. Then your heart gets lined up with the enthusiasm needed to propel it to success. After you have accomplished your hopes and dreams, make a new list as soon as possible. Remain full of hope throughout this life. If not for yourself, be hopeful for others to just keep hope alive.

The Past Has Passed.
Leave It There.

The Blessings of the Lord cannot be received if you are looking back at your past life. That life will contaminate every good blessing God has for you. The past has passed. Leave it there and move on and get prepared for all of the wonderful things God has prepared for you. God does not operate on your time, my time, or any time at all. No, he operates in seasons. This is the season that many have awaited, the one when God will restore the years the locust and the cankerworms have eaten. Surely, God knows what you need and what you hope for, so get prepared to receive God's best now. Clean out your closet and get ready to receive new garments within and without. You will now receive the garments of salvation, the robe of righteousness, the garment of praise for the spirit of heaviness (Isaiah 61). Notice that "garments" is plural. Yes, the people of God will have many glorious materials and spiritual garments as well. The garments of praise for the spirit of heaviness, the spirit of joy and gladness after their trials. Once you have the eternal garments on, you can select your designer of choice, (i.e. Ralph, Oscar, Louis, Gucci, Coach, etc.). After all of the battles and trials of life, the glorified outer garments may seem a bit contrived, yet they will be available at your request. With all of the great plans God has for your life, why would you dwell on the past? The past has passed. Leave it there.

Thy Will Be Done
My Will Be Done

Operating from the will of God or from our own will brings us to different events and circumstances of life. Without God as a guidepost, our will leads us around the mulberry bush, aimlessly wandering from one experience to another. It's interesting that choices are made from what appeared to be right for us however turned out to be completely wrong in the end. God's will for our lives is so much greater than what we can imagine with our limited minds. Handing over our will unties God's hand to build a life much greater than any we could build with our own power and will. The human nature that is separated from God operates from its own will. This produces endless circular experiences that seem to always end up on the same street. Submitting to God's will require great humility. Mary was humbled in submission to God's will and conceived our savior. Jesus humbled himself in his Father's request that he be sacrificed for all mankind. Humility is a must in the daily walk of Christians, as we know the mighty and awesome power of God. Knowing that we are connected to someone greater than ourselves and that we were formed by that greatness is very humbling. God gave everyone the gift of free will, so the choice is ours to make. There will be no force or coercion, because God wants us to freely choose whom we shall serve. Thy will be done, or my will be done. Make your own choice.

It Was In The Cup

In the Garden of Gethsemane, Jesus drank the cup of the abomination for all mankind. Every sin that had been committed before and that would be committed after was in the cup. What love God had for mankind that he would ransom his beloved son to save souls. This moment in the garden was the only time Jesus became separated from God, as the Holy Spirit of God could not abide in him with the presence of sin. Being fully human at the time, he felt anguish, alienation, and loneliness. His human nature pleaded with God to take the cup from him. His divine nature replied, "Not my will but thy will be done." When circumstances of life are disturbing to you, stop for a moment and tell yourself, "That was in the cup." If someone is rude and disrespectful to you, just take a breath and tell yourself that all of him or her was in the cup, too. Have a chuckle and carry on. Remember this when unexpected phone calls that take your peace and joy. Yes, you are getting good at it now. You know the rest. It was in the cup. Ignorance about the magnitude of that sacrifice is keeping many people in bondage. Jesus is waiting for us to cast that weight and burden on him. He is the power, and he is empowered to lift it from us so that we can be free. Give none of the abominations of this day any credence or credibility. Remember that "it was all in the cup." Make sure that you are taking full advantage of such a loving sacrifice, and live your life in freedom and wholeness.

The God Of Special Effects

The field of entertainment relies heavily on the element of special effects. Special effects are designed to appear larger than life and border on the impossible. People want to be wowed by the seemingly impossible and be lifted from the monotony of everyday living. Our God is the ultimate master of special effects that last forever. Man has been endowed with many gifts from God with which to create one's reality in this world. Given such great abilities to become self-sufficient, sometimes God has to use special effects to get our attention. In the book of Exodus, God frees his people from Egypt by means of special effects. Remember the ten plagues that finally set the Israelites free. Wow! What about the Red Sea parting for them to cross? Wow! The Israelites were in the desert then, with no food or water. How did they survive? God sent manna and quail and split a rock for a continuous flow of Poland Springs water. Wow! Wow! Wow! After all of the wonderful special effects and assistance given to his people, many remained in rebellion and disobedience to the laws and ordinances given to them. The Lord always saves the best for last, and truly, the birth of his son, Jesus, sent to redeem and restore mankind, was the ultimate special effect. After his baptism by John and the Holy Spirit, showtime began. The lame, the blind, those possessed by demons, and the dead were all restored to new life. Wow! Wow! Wow! Wow! A life given over to God is a life that enters the cinema of special effects. Sorry, the lights stay on, because your future becomes brighter and brighter. You won't need the Milk Duds or the popcorn. You will be fed by God's love. Abundant joy will be your daily food.

The Doing Mind
The Being Heart

The human mind was wired for thinking and doing, for achieving and accomplishing the task at hand. In the daily process of doing, we must remember to establish our being as well. Our being is synonymous with our attitude. What attitude—hopefully positive— keeps our spirits lifted. The essence of being needs to be expressed for flow and harmony in the life. Establishing and maintaining your being should come first so that your doing can be more rewarding and efficient. Make a conscientious decision about your daily being, whether peaceful, kind, generous, positive, or present in all of life's moments. Our minds are sometimes in a hurry to complete a task while the heart wants excitement, happiness, and laughter. The issues of life are experienced in the heart. Therefore, we must think with our heads and live from our hearts. If the heart has been affected or infected by past experiences, there first must come healing in order for your life to flow easier. Negative experiences of the past can hold your heart in bondage and rob you of the joy of living. Once the heart is healed, the love can flow within and out to your world. The healing process is not easy, because it requires forgiveness of those past hurtful experiences. We have all been forgiven for every sin past, present, and future by Christ's sacrifice on the cross. Although he experienced great suffering from abandonment, he still forgave mankind. Jesus forgave all on the cross when he said, "Father forgive them: for they know not what they do." Given our own power, it can be difficult to forgive; however, we can pray for the gift of forgiveness. Now that the issues of the past are resolved, you can express the heart of love and the mind of peace.

Walking Testimony

I am a walking testimony of the power of God to heal, renew, and restore a life. When there is a purpose and a destiny to the life of the believer, it does not matter what you experienced. You will rise as the victor, not the victim. It is the same testimony for all of God's children in this life. We survive the deaths of loved ones, failed marriages, ill health, and the list goes on. The one overwhelming fact is that we are not destroyed in the battle. While we are going through life, God is destroying things in us that are in the way of our salvation. Yes, you will feel like you are constantly laboring; however, you will deliver the baby and soon forget all the pains of delivery. While you were in the battle, God was working behind the scenes, rearranging the furniture and changing the landscape. It may appear that the weight of adversity was bigger than you and that there was no way around it, but you got over it eventually. Yes, I am a walking testimony of the power of God to strengthen you in the battle and keep you unshakeable, unmovable, and unstoppable. I can't remember one tear through it all. As a soldier of God, I could not fight and cry at the same time. There are some children of God made for the battles, warriors by nature. These are God's Judah children, warriors and soldiers of the cross. There comes a time when you must step aside and come in from the battles. God will let you know when to let a hardship go, and at that moment, God will deliver the last and final blow to the enemy. We don't know all of the nooks and crannies of the enemy, but God knows them all, past and future. Now that you have stepped aside, God can begin to restore you, renew you, and revive you to new life. Yes, I am a walking testimony of God's love, mercy, goodness, and faithfulness to his children. What a mighty God I serve.

A Glorious, Daily Christmas

Joyful spirits are equated with the Christmas season. People seem more alive, more charitable, and kinder to one another. It is the season of exchanging lovely gifts, giving best wishes, and enjoying glorious decorations and meals together. The real reason we celebrate the season sometimes gets lost among the fast commercialism of the event. This is the established birthday of God's ultimate gift to mankind, his son, Jesus. Daily thankfulness puts you in the right spirit to receive God's continuous Christmas gifts. God wants you to enjoy all of the toys he gives you and to share them with the less fortunate. This will make for a continuous flow of your blessings and the keys to God's eternal toy chest. Celebration should not be based solely on calendar events but rather the celebration of living and being free without limitations. Celebrate God's sacrifice. Share his love with your brothers and sisters around the world. Celebrate his victory for you and me on calvary and live **A GLORIOUS AND DAILY CHRISTMAS.**

Etiquette Beyond Tea

The idea of etiquette brings to mind a beautifully decorated table with ladies at tea, holding their tea cups with their pinkies extended and drinking imported tea. Today, etiquette has gone beyond the tea parties; however, it still includes them as well. It can be a very powerful tool in this age of globalization, especially in homes, churches, temples, schools, and businesses. It is important to be aware of the customs of other countries as well as the customs of our own and the character these should establish and portray. The principles of etiquette are ancient; however, the need for this discipline has come full circle now. During those days, it had nothing to do with tea at all, but it concerned a need to established proper behavior for the development of the sons of Egyptian kings. The queen, of course, would guide and teach their daughters the necessary etiquette principles of the royal courts. Etiquette goes beyond one's social or economic status, because it helps for successful navigation in life. One's behavior and proper presentation can open many doors that may otherwise be closed. With competition for employment, learning about the proper dress, correct posture, and presentation would obviously be to an applicant's advantage and give them the edge he or she may need. Although etiquette has gone beyond tea, the tea party is where the fun was. In by gone days, ladies would dress in their beautiful apparel and have afternoon tea together. They would select a topic of conversation that included everyone at the table and sip tea creating an atmosphere of tranquility. This daily ritual has come again in some hotels and restaurants, which adds another dimension of service for customers who can remember The Golden Age of Tea service and for those who would now like to experience it for the first time. All can benefit from etiquette and enjoy the Tea Party.

Kindness, The Priceless Key

Kindness can open many doors that would normally be closed to you. The right look, social status, and family name may have opened doors for you in the past. These are all surface qualities that do not reflect who you really are inside. In some cases, genuine kindness can override great credentials, because it is often important to hire a person who contributes to the well-being of the staff while he or she can be proficient on the job, too. The positive energy from an act of kindness puts you in a higher energy field. It can even restore health and well-being. The person or persons receiving the special gift of your kindness benefit from it as well; however, you benefit doubly, because your heart as well as your spirit is engaged. On some days, you may have a difficult time maintaining positive energy, because the negative outside is constantly trying to dictate to you. On these days, you must fight for your positive energy even harder and persist in kindness even in the face of the unkind. This is a Christian principle that is truly very difficult, for our flesh wants to fight back; however, when we employ our Holy Spirit, we are given the necessary strength to retain our peace and composure. Now, here is what most people have issues with: You must be intently kind whether or not you receive that kindness in return. As a child of God, you will have to keep working on that principle until you master it. Kindness suggests that love is present, the greatest power of all the powers that can transform the giver and the receiver. Love won long ago with the loving sacrifice on the cross of calvary, and love was the last commandment Jesus gave his disciples. Embrace the kindness within you and realize that it is a wonderful power that you can use to change your world.

About the Author

Navigate Life's Journey was written from a life-long experience of navigating Alexandra's own life with divine assistance and great faith in a power greater than us all. One must live the experience in order to be a beacon of hope for others in need of direction. Alexandra states that there is no need to expound on any of her personal experiences as her experiences are the same as every ones. She explains that all have experienced lost family, lost friends, lost loves, lost jobs, lost dreams however she never experienced lost faith nor lost hope. Alexandra hopes that this book will speak to and propel the readers to new heights of encouragement and inspiration. Her University Degrees were obtained in Psychology and Sociology from The City University of New York in 1975. Alexandra was employed thirty years with the U.S. Federal Government and has since retired. Recently she obtained certifications from The Academy of Etiquette and Protocol of Orlando, Florida and The International Etiquette and Protocol Academy of London, England. Alexandra has established The Westchester Royal Academy of Etiquette and Protocol located in the lovely village of Bronxville, New York. Her classes are currently held in the grand historical house of The Bronxville

Women's Club. The classes are designed to build self confidence, manners, social skills and character. She expressed that it is an honor to be part of the domestic and global helping hands to guide the youth in a positive direction.